Seb and the Cat

By Sally Cowan

Seb can see rats.

The rats ran to a tin can.

The rats fit in the can.

Seb can see a man.

It is Ben.

Ben can see Seb.

Ben hit the pan!

A cat can see Seb.

Seb can see it.

To the pit, Seb!

The cat taps at the pit.

Seb can fit in his pit.

Seb sits.

CHECKING FOR MEANING

1. What is Seb looking for? *(Literal)*

2. Where did Seb go when the cat saw him? *(Literal)*

3. Why did Ben hit the pan? *(Inferential)*

EXTENDING VOCABULARY

can	Find the word *can* in the text. Does it always have the same meaning? What are the two meanings of this word?
rats	Look at the word *rats*. Take away the *s* at the end of the word. What is the new word? How is the meaning different to the word *rats*?
fit	What is the meaning of the word *fit* in *The rats fit in the can*?

MOVING BEYOND THE TEXT

1. What do snakes eat?

2. What would you do if you saw a snake on the ground? Why?

3. How do you think Seb felt when he saw the cat? Why?

4. Why do some snakes live under the ground?

SPEED SOUNDS

| Cc | Bb | Rr | Ee | Ff | Hh | Nn |

| Mm | Ss | Aa | Pp | Ii | Tt |

Seb

can

ran

tin

rats

man

fit

Man

in

Hit

Ben

pan

hit

Cat

Pan

Rats

cat